Praise for *Re-Thin*

"*Re-Thinking Humility* is essential reading for leaders at all levels in every sector of business, government and non-profits. This book offers practical research, tools and anecdotes to demonstrate how embracing a servant leader ethos and sharing the stage can build stronger, more resilient teams and organizations."

—Penny Pritzker, Chairman and Founder of PSP Partners and former
U.S. Commerce Secretary

"In a time when more and more leaders are using their position as a platform to enhance their own celebrity, often to the detriment of their organizations, Doug Hensch's book on the benefits of humility is like a cool drink in the hot desert. Inside this small but powerful book, leaders will find a solid discussion of humility itself, and some super-useful tools to help leaders become more effective by recognizing the truth."

—ADM John Richardson, USN (Ret), 31st Chief of Naval Operations

"We need more leaders to roll up their sleeves and activate the timeless virtue of humility. *Re-Thinking Humility* is a terrific reminder about actions, consequences, feelings and results. This practical, research-based book offers a concise, easy-to-read plan for bringing more humility and better results to your organization."

—Tony Nader, Co–Founder & Managing Director, SWaN & Legend Venture Partners; Vice Chairman, Asurion

"Humility is a sign of leader's strength. It takes courage to admit that you don't have all the answers and that you need the support of others. Such openness draws followers to the leader because they feel they can make a strong contribution to the team. Doug Hensch maps out the reasons for humility and means for implementing it. *Re-Thinking Humility* is a go-to book on this important topic."

—John Baldoni, Global Guru in Leadership, member of 100 Coaches and author of 15 books including *Grace Notes: Leading in an Upside-Down World* and *Lead with Purpose: Getting the Organization to Believe in Itself*

"This is a delightful read coupled with a deep exploration of an essential ingredient of being human. It's full of stories that go straight to the head and heart. Truly illuminating!"

—Joy Leach, President, PRI Leadership

"Leadership really, really matters, and Doug Hensch has given us an important book at an important time. In this era of divisiveness and distrust, *Re-Thinking Humility* is a key to effective leadership in our troubled times."

—Bill Novelli, professor at Georgetown University's McDonough School of Business, former CEO of AARP and president, Porter Novelli, is the author of *Good Business: The Talk, Fight, Win Way to Change the World.*

"Humility is a critical trait for leaders and it's more complicated than saying "we" more often. Doug Hensch enlightens us to the why and how of what great leaders understand about it."

—L. David Marquet, former nuclear submarine commander, author of *Turn the Ship Around!*

"I was struck early-on when reading *Re-Thinking Humility* when an inspiring quote from Maya Angelou was followed a page or two later by a line from a Will Ferrell movie—author Doug Hensch throws a wide net, and we as readers are all the richer for it. Doug has both an insatiable curiosity and an encyclopedic mind that are not just open to but actively plugged into leaders, writers, thinkers and researchers in countless fields around the world. In his latest book, *Re-Thinking Humility*, Doug has given us as readers, learners, and leaders a fast-paced and actionable executive summary of humility—what it is, why its development is so urgent, and—most importantly—what we can each do to bring about this much needed skillset. Drawn from best practices and lessons learned across the fields of business, military service, sports, entertainment, and others, Doug's examples are current, real and immediately accessible. While containing timeless wisdom an insight, *Re-Thinking Humility* is finding us when we—our families, our businesses, and our culture—need humility more than ever."

—Hile Rutledge, President and Principal Consultant, OKA

"*Re-Thinking Humility* helped me re-consider the role that this essential virtue plays in leadership and life. Doug Hensch gives us a practical, easy-to-read outline of what it takes to build great leaders. Full of anecdotes, research and tips, *Re-Thinking Humility* is a go-to book!"

— Anne Loehr, SVP, Center for Human Capital innovation

"When I read Doug's works I find both my "real self" and my "aspirational self" - I am both challenged and inspired by the insights, concepts and thought leadership Doug brings to his writing. *Re-Thinking Humility* takes us on a kind of guided reflection that delivers practical application strategies even as we examine our own relationship with humility. To me, you can't ask for more than a book that inspires deep thought and motivates practical application - and that's Doug's signature."

—Daniel Porter

Re-Thinking Humility

Getting Back To An Essential Ingredient
of Great Leadership

Doug Hensch

Published by DRH Media

Printed and bound in the United States of America

ISBN: 978-1-7365682-0-0

To Mom & Dad
Thank you for your unconditional love and support.
You've always kept me grounded.

Table of Contents

Preface

"Be humble, for you are made of earth. Be noble,
for you are made of stars."
—Serbian proverb

I set up a meeting with prolific author and top-notch executive coach John Baldoni in the spring of 2021 to get some advice on writing my next book. John had been on my podcast to talk about his latest book, *Grace: A Leader's Guide to a Better Us*, and I really respected the way that he approached the topic of leadership. I told him that I wanted to write something about humility that would be useful and practical for leaders. I figured this would take at least three to four years to write because of the extensive research I would need to do.

"I'm sorry, Doug," John replied after I told him my goal and how long I expected it to take. "That's just not going to cut it. The world needs this book now. We can't wait four more years." And, with that comment, this turned into an 83 page paperback that won't be on any best-selling list other than my own!

So began the sprint to get this book out as quickly as possible, with just a few guidelines. First, I wanted it to be practical. Feel free to skip to Chapter 6, "How do we get more of it?" if all you're interested in are the tips, tools, and exercises to build humility. I won't be offended. Second, I wanted this to be based on research and the wisdom of people I admired. I interviewed a number of humble leaders, and (as you might guess) they often do not like to speak about themselves. I quickly combed through the research and coerced a handful of humble leaders and amazing coaches to satisfy my curiosity. Next, I wanted it to be readable. Stories and anecdotes make research come alive. I find them inspiring, and I hope you do, too.

The hardest part of writing this, though, was defining humility. If I went with the simple version (humility = modesty), this would be a *really* short book without a lot of value. Modesty is a big part of it, but it doesn't do humility justice. In the end, I settled on a version of the definition from the late Chris Peterson that has four separate components: (1) the need or desire to stay in the background (this is what most people think of when they ponder the definition of humility), (2) a focus on the needs of others, (3) being accurate when assessing your abilities (quite often, people think humility is thinking *less* of yourself), and (4) allowing others to influence you. This definition supercharged my motivation. Now I had a robust concept that I could explore from multiple angles.

And these angles kept surprising me. Right as I was beginning the last few chapters, I learned another lesson. My wife (Tammy) and I had a small disagreement that turned into a big fight that lasted longer than I am willing to admit. In short, I knew I was right. I stopped listening. I was the definition of arrogance. Then, I sat down to write Chapter 6 and I realized just how arrogant I was being in this context. Embarrassed doesn't even begin to describe how I felt when I figured it out. *How can I write a book on humility and act like such an ass?* I asked myself a couple of questions (again, from Chapter 6), and that opened the door to a dialogue that helped us figure it out. Honestly, this breakthrough doesn't happen without a dose of humility …

Another event from earlier in the year actually inspired me to get writing. My oldest son (Nick) is in the Junior Naval ROTC program at his high school. At the end of the junior year, there is a traditional naval warfare game where the cadets get a chance to practice some of the strategies and tactics they have learned in the past three years of training and classwork. One day at the end of the school year, Nick told me that he had been elected as commander of one of the teams. I congratulated him, told him how proud I was, and asked him a few questions. "How did you earn this rank?" I asked.

"My classmates elected me," Nick said. Then he added, "And the funny thing is that I didn't even vote for myself. I'm really nervous about leading a team. I just don't want to fail."

"Nick, I think I'm even more proud of you for that than for your being elected commander," I said. I then told him about how George Washington and Chester Nimitz confided to their wives that they weren't sure if they were up to the task and that they never bragged about their power. Both were highly respected by those they commanded, and both served their country brilliantly.

Because he had the humility to admit that he had a gap in his knowledge about leading, he asked for my advice about going about this. Nick also read up on the Battle of Midway and several other important naval engagements to be ready for what the "enemy" threw at him. All of this was motivated by a sense of humility. In the end, he gained a great deal of confidence from this experience. (In case you're wondering, Nick's team won!)

There is no single skill, strength, or virtue that makes great leaders. Leadership is a complex undertaking, and you will find no shortage of books on the subject. After speaking with a number of respected, successful leaders, coaches, and consultants, I am convinced that the multifaceted, emotional issues we face economically, environmentally, and politically are virtually unsolvable without a healthy dose of humility, especially from those who are given the honor of leading. My hope for you is that you will find a couple of useful tips and tools to make you a better leader and maybe an interesting story or two to share with others.

Chapter 1
What Is Humility?

"Humility is truth."—St. Theresa of Avila

During my high school years, my best friend and I were consumed with our love of football (that is, the American version with helmets, shoulder pads, and Super Bowls). He was our starting wide receiver and I was the quarterback, so we spent hours playing catch, watching games, and trying to build muscle in the weight room. My buddy's dad, John Hock, was a Pro-Bowl offensive lineman for the Los Angeles Rams in the 1950s. Mr. Hock knew that his son (Jim) and I were trying to gain weight, so he routinely asked me when I walked in the front door of their house, "Doug, want a milkshake?" The answer was rarely no.

One night in the summer of 1986, I entered their house and walked directly into the kitchen. The smoky, savory smell of bacon-and-egg sandwiches filled the room. As a growing teenager, I was ready to eat, and my eyes locked on to these heavenly snacks. Mr. Hock noticed my gaze. Instead of offering me a creamy, homemade milkshake, he didn't hesitate and graciously offered, "Those sandwiches are yours if you want them, Doug." I said, "Thank you," and put them away in record time.

Shortly after I finished, Mrs. Hock entered the kitchen and began talking to her husband about his long day at work and asked if he had eaten his bacon-and-egg sandwiches yet. She knew he had been working extra long hours lately and wanted to make sure he was fed. He winked at me and said, "Yeah, Micki, they really hit the spot. Thank you."

Needless to say, I felt really selfish for eating Mr. Hock's dinner. However, that was John Hock. He *thought of others just as much as or more than he thought about himself.* He was a true servant leader and one of the kindest people I've ever known.

As for his pro football career, you would never know he played unless you really paid attention. He had a slight stoop in his back and a limp that can be attributed to multiple knee operations after his six-year career in the NFL. In 1955, John Hock was awarded the game ball for the Western Conference Championship (an incredibly rare feat for an offensive lineman), which was signed by all of his teammates, several of whom were enshrined in the Pro Football Hall of Fame in Canton, Ohio. What would you do with this football if it were awarded to you? If you said, display it prominently on the mantel, you would have made a different choice than Mr. Hock. He let his two youngest boys use it to play catch in the backyard. As you might imagine, most of the names are now hard to read, and the football looks worn out and ordinary. That was also John Hock. You see, Mr. Hock *never bragged.* In fact, when someone tried to brag about him, he often just smiled or laughed, then changed the subject.

John Hock is a perfect example of the first two elements of Dr. Chris Peterson's definition of humility: (1) relatively low self-focus or an ability to "forget the self," and (2) lacking a strong desire or need to be the center of attention. And, just like your favorite info-mercial … *Wait, there's more!*

Another great example of a more nuanced look at humility is David Marquet, a retired submarine commander and leadership coach. In one of my favorite books on leadership, *Turn the Ship Around!—A True Story of Turning Followers into Leaders*, Marquet shares his story of making a number of mistakes and then listening to his officers to completely change the way he led his submarine as he demonstrates the last two elements of Peterson's definition.

Marquet was not incompetent by any means. In fact, he graduated from the United States Naval Academy near the top of his class and earned his command from years of proven leadership. The problem was that he had been training for a different class of submarine before he took command of the *Santa Fe*. After roughly a year of preparing for a certain class of sub, he was assigned to the *Santa Fe*, the worst-performing sub in the Pacific at the time. Marquet had never been aboard this class of submarine as well as the one he had diligently trained for, so naturally, he gave some orders that the crew just could not execute. (In one almost striking example, he ordered "All ahead two-thirds!" And, this particular submarine did not have a "two-thirds" setting, so the helmsman just froze and did nothing!) He saw the pattern in his behavior and *became aware of his abilities and knowledge* as they related to this particular sub.

Over the course of many conversations with his team of officers, Marquet *listened to his team* and changed his entire approach by ceasing to give orders. His officers would engage him by saying, "I intend to.." Together, they developed a language of sharing "intentions" that propelled the *Santa Fe* to the highest performance rating ever for a submarine in the Pacific Fleet. None of this would have been possible had he tried to fake his way to knowing more about the sub when he didn't. And, by listening to his crew, he helped create a team culture that completely turned it around. He created an entire submarine of leaders.

Marquet describes his mindset as "care, don't care." Care deeply and passionately about the team and the mission and don't care about the bureaucratic consequences to yourself. In fact, he told me that he often imagined that he'd already been fired which freed him from any expectations and allowed him to focus his entire energy on what the team needed.

The final two pieces of Dr. Peterson's definition—(3) accurately assessing one's abilities and (4) being open to the influence of others—are demonstrated by Marquet's command of the *Santa Fe.* The majority of the book you're reading now will focus on how humility is the catalyst for becoming a better leader.

"Humility is not thinking less of yourself,
it's thinking of yourself less."
—Rick Warren

When I set out to write about humility, my goal was to offer some research and strategies around creating a kinder society and better leaders through modesty. I admire people who achieve greatness and just refuse to brag or boast while giving credit to others. And, one of my first tasks was to look for a definition that could do it justice. What I learned was that we're just scratching the surface of the power of humility when we limit it to "not bragging" and "being modest."

Most people believe (as I did) that the definition of humility is the same as modesty. Yet, per Peterson's definition, it's only one element. And modesty is only what we see on the outside. True humility is on the inside, which brings up an important point. Therefore, I believe it is very difficult to determine if someone else is truly humble, at least when it comes to judging by modesty. In some sense, we can only prove the negative—if we see a significant amount of bragging and attempts to be the center of attention, we can safely say this person is low on this component of humility. If we see, for instance, a leader telling the media that "All the accolades belong to the team …," it may be a learned behavior. This leader may be reading her audience and thinking, "It's time to show some humility even though this team couldn't have done it without me."

This focus on modesty is understandable since the word "humble" is derived from the Latin words *humus*, meaning "ground" or "earth," and *humilis*, meaning "low" or "lowly." With these origins, it's probably easy to see why most people tend to think of those who are humble as having a low opinion of themselves. My interviews for the research of this book began with leaders, executive coaches, and trusted colleagues offering this point as their definition of humility. Usually, "not bragging" was seen as the top quality, or "staying out of the limelight." Others reported that humble people aren't "ball hogs" (a player in a team sport who keeps the ball as they try to score on their own).

As we take a deeper dive, it may be helpful to label these four elements in a way that's a little easier to remember. A good way to keep this definition of humility in mind is with the acronym HELP.

H – Head backstage; leave the center stage, accolades, and attention for others

E – Empathize and focus on others before thinking about yourself

L – List your abilities accurately

P – Permit others to influence you

This chapter began with the words of Saint Theresa of Avila, "Humility is truth." Admiral (Ret.) John Richardson, Chief Naval Officer of the United States Navy from 2015 to 2019, shared these words with me one hot day in July of 2021 as we talked about the role of humility in leadership. If acronyms are not for you, just remember this quote, because each element of the definition brings us closer to the "truth." Clamoring for attention and recognition prevents you from truly listening and understanding. Focusing on yourself first masks the truth and gives you only one small piece of the picture. Being able to accurately assess your skills and abilities allows you to take on challenges that match your capabilities. Allowing others to influence us makes for smarter decisions and an expanded knowledge base. Truth may be just a dose of humility away.

As we dig into this ancient virtue, I hope to make it clear that humility is not a magic bullet for great leadership. Becoming a great leader is a difficult, sometimes complex, undertaking. My argument is that while it may not be the cure-all that leaders are seeking, it is essential for making a positive, lasting difference.

Re-Thinking Humility

Chapter 2
So What?

"Humility, that low, sweet root,
from which all heavenly virtues shoot."
—Thomas Moore

"I'm so proud of this guy for what he's done this year, I can't even tell you," Alabama head football coach Nick Saban said as he hugged quarterback Jalen Hurts with his voice trailing off after his team beat rival Georgia in an emotional 2018 SEC Championship. Saban was overtaken by emotion after watching his quarterback lead the team to victory. He is considered by some to be the greatest college football coach of all time and someone who doesn't regularly show a significant amount of emotion—unless, of course, it's anger when a player doesn't perfectly execute his complex scheme. In this particular case, Coach Saban was in awe of this young man and inspired by his performance.

I've played this game and watched hundreds (maybe thousands) of sports interviews at this point in my life. I remember this moment so clearly because I also watched Alabama play Georgia in the previous season's epic national championship when Hurts was benched by none other than Nick Saban.

Hurts arrived on the Alabama campus in 2016 as a top recruit. Tall, quiet, and blessed with a cannon for an arm and a boundless work ethic, he quietly earned the starting quarterback role as a freshman. He was unassuming and didn't draw a lot of attention to himself. A touchdown pass was usually met with a quick, head-down jog to the sidelines, almost as if to say, "OK, don't look at me. It was a team effort."

He won a bunch of awards and helped guide the team to the national championship game against then upstart Clemson in 2017. In a game for the ages with multiple lead changes, heroic plays, devastating tackles, and screaming fans, Hurts gave his best, and yet it still wasn't enough. The Alabama offense sputtered when it needed to be efficient, and his completion percentage was well below what is considered even average. Crimson Tide fans were getting restless and beginning to talk about a change at quarterback.

Not one to be flustered, Hurts entered the following season as the presumed starter. And, because Alabama is so incredibly talented, they routinely beat teams by 30 or more points, which gives the backups plenty of playing time. This included a dynamic freshman with a huge smile, swagger, and a penchant for big plays named Tua Tagovailoa.

Alabama fans were excited to see their team once again in the national championship game, this time against their conference rival Georgia. Unfortunately, it was one of Hurts' worst performances. The vaunted Alabama offense that routinely scored 30 points in a half couldn't muster a measly field goal. They were down 13–0 after the first 30 minutes of play. Saban decided to make a gutsy move and change quarterbacks. Tua was now leading the offense and Alabama roared back to outscore Georgia 20–7 in the second half and force overtime, where they eventually won the game 26–23.

As I watched this game, I couldn't help but feel profound sorrow for Jalen Hurts. It's one thing to get pulled in the biggest game of the year with tens of millions of fans watching on TV. It's another to see your backup make great plays and throw a perfect 41-yard pass to win the game—in this case the national championship.

I kept looking for Hurts on the sideline. I was curious to see how he would react, as I've watched other benched players stand or sit, looking disinterested, angry, or just plain sad. Quite frankly, I'm not sure that I could blame someone who is only 19 or 20 years old for being a little self-consumed in a moment like this with millions of eyes upon them. (I've seen plenty of professional players throw tantrums on the field for being taken out or not agreeing with coaching decisions.) Hurts would have none of it. He was jumping up and down, cheering every big play by his team. He urged his 'Bama teammates to focus and give their all. Players coming off the field (including Tua) were the recipients of congratulatory high fives, bear hugs, and encouraging words from Jalen Hurts.

When it was over, Hurts was celebrating just like everyone else, like a little kid as the obligatory confetti fell from the sky and cameras rushed onto the field with reporters eager to interview Tua, his teammates, and Coach Saban. No pouting whatsoever.

In the following weeks, I expected to hear that Hurts would transfer so that he could get two more years of college experience before entering the National Football League's annual draft. He decided to stay at Alabama and share time with Tua—with Tua starting most games. All season long, Jalen Hurts gave high fives, pats on the back, and never said a discouraging word to the press.

Again, Alabama had a fantastic season, and just before the national playoffs, Tua seriously injured his ankle against Georgia in the SEC Championship. Saban put Hurts in, and all the young quarterback did was run, pass, and will his team to win. Make no mistake, I'm not an Alabama fan by any means. But I became a Jalen Hurts fan that day. When the game was over, Nick Saban must have been feeling what I and—I'm guessing—millions of others were feeling. It was a potent cocktail of awe, inspiration, love, and admiration for this young man. And, when I saw Coach Saban getting choked up, it was easy to see that Jalen Hurts was a special young man who literally led from behind.

OK, so Jalen Hurts inspired me and thousands of other fans. What makes this so important? *So what?*

"Humility is the antithesis of entitlement."—John Baldoni

Baldoni, author of *Grace: A Leader's Guide to a Better Us*, also writes that humility opens us up to understanding. What if Jalen Hurts had focused on his own situation and disregarded the program? What if he had complained to reporters and teammates? Of course, we'll never know the answers to these hypothetical scenarios. What we do know, however, is that Jalen Hurts built trust with the coaching staff and his teammates by *understanding* where he stood on this team and that the team came first. He energized his team and rallied them when they needed him most not by giving a fiery speech or demanding to play. He inspired a talented group of individuals by *not* drawing attention to himself all season, by focusing on others before himself and recognizing the truth—that Tua was the starter and (maybe) he was the right guy for the job.

Hurts demonstrated some of the benefits of leading with humility. After exploring the research, interviewing multiple leadership experts, and poring over my notes, I believe the benefits of leading with humility are akin to the ripple we see in a pond with that first drop of rain. The still water is transformed into a growing circle that starts with just one small drop and grows into larger and larger circles that reach well beyond the original point of impact. Humility starts with *Self*, impacts the immediate *Team* you are leading, and reaches outward to the rest of the *Organization* and beyond.

SELF

Humility helps us see the world more accurately. Baldoni also writes that it "opens the door to self-understanding." Truly understanding ourselves gives us the space to see our capabilities as they are and not necessarily as we want them to be. Understanding Self does not need to be a positive or negative judgment. It is simply a mindful view in which the goal is objectivity. And, objectivity is hard to achieve without humility.

Shannon Polly has a master's degree in Applied Positive Psychology from the University of Pennsylvania. She is a Professional Certified Coach through the International Coach Federation and she co-edited *Character Strengths Matter—How to Live a Full Life*. She argues that humility is a catalyst for curiosity. She posits that humility helps us understand that we may not have all the answers to a particular problem. Curiosity propels us to seek new information, to engage with our colleagues and seek out information without bias.

I would argue that part of the benefit to Self is that humility is a catalyst for a number of character strengths beyond curiosity, which include:

- **Creativity**—This is one of the most important strengths of our era. Finding ways to generate new and useful ideas is the cornerstone of great problem-solving and innovation. Humility's role is to help us understand that true creativity allows us to sit with some bad ideas before the good ones emerge.
- **Gratitude**—It is one of the most studied and useful character strengths. Study after study shows that gratitude links to higher levels of resilience and well-being. Humility can activate gratitude by helping us see what is good in the world beyond ourselves.
- **Open-Mindedness**—Humans are judging machines. We gather information, and our biases and judgment-making

machinery are in full throttle. Humility reminds us to "slow down to speed up" and consider what other points of view may add to our own wisdom and knowledge.

- **Empathy**—Our ability to put ourselves in others' shoes is critical to being a great leader. Satya Nadella, CEO of Microsoft, often talks about empathy as foundational for leading in any realm. Again, humility helps us put the focus on others rather than ourselves.

Dan Porter, executive coach and talented author, asserts that humility is the beginning of a virtuous cycle that starts with Self. When the leader has the "perspective that [they are] no greater or lesser" than anyone on the team, they are planting the seeds of true teamwork—where the whole is greater than the sum of its parts.

Building on this idea, leading with humility drastically reduces the pressure a leader can feel. When the leader is the person with all the answers, the team begins to draw the leader into too many decisions. As a result, this pressure makes some leaders lose sleep, lose their temper, and lose their effectiveness.

TEAM

Think about your immediate team for a moment—the small group that relies on each other to get work done, meets regularly, etc. How would you describe the culture? How does the team get along? How well does the team collaborate? What happens when there is disagreement? The answers to these questions are often proportional to the degree of humility exhibited by the team's leader.

In one study from the University of Washington Foster School of Business, leaders who scored higher on humility (as rated by their colleagues) had teams with individuals who were more engaged with their work and less likely to leave the organization. The co-author of the study, Michael Johnson, PhD, argues that humble leaders are "the people who are behind the scenes, guiding their employees and letting them shine." Johnson also writes, "Our study suggests that a 'quieter' leadership approach— listening, being transparent, being aware of limitations, and appreciating follower strengths and contributions—is an effective way to engage employees."

It is then not too great a stretch to say that when a leader sets the tone for the team by not dominating the conversations, focusing on others, and being open to influence, you have a team that is more likely to follow in these footsteps. There is a cascading effect that results in norms that produce a psychologically safe environment where people feel free to share whatever is on their mind. Diversity in thought leads to higher levels of innovation, better problem-solving, improved decision-making, and enhanced morale.

My coaching process often starts with a "360-degree review" where I interview employees who work with my client. Most coaches today send out online surveys that ask over 100 questions and produce pretty graphs with normative data that help executives see how they stand versus their peers. What these electronic surveys don't tell you is how deep the loyalty, respect, and admiration for my clients can run. Listening for the passion in followership gives me just a little more data to paint a more accurate picture of the leader.

When a client is humble, I hear it in the voices of the people who report directly to them. The employees are effusive in their praise. They talk about the selflessness of their leader, how she "rolls up her sleeves," or how he listens and how she cares. They often share stories about their leader making sure other people get credit for big accomplishments. And the most popular anecdotes usually relate to how well the team is performing. They cite instances where disagreement leads to better decisions and conflict actually strengthens their bonds. Often, it's not the behaviors of the leader they share, it's the success of the team—just the way the humble leader prefers.

ORGANIZATION

**"Arrogance is a mental illness that
stops you from performing."
—Alan Robinson**

In 1997, I was working for a startup in the telecommunications industry. I was employee number 17 in a company that eventually had over 500 people in its ranks, so I was able to watch the organization grow from almost nothing to being acquired by a well-known telecommunications giant. As the company grew, I watched as we struggled to innovate, solve problems, and differentiate our offerings in a fast-moving industry. While a few executives at the top of the organization became wealthy from the acquisition, most of the employees didn't get rich. I also noticed we were missing a sense of higher purpose throughout the company. This fueled my curiosity about what was missing and what leaders could do about it.

Sometime that same year, I stumbled on *Corporate Creativity— How Innovation and Improvement Actually Happen* by Alan Robinson and Sam Stern. I was fascinated by what the most creative companies were doing to generate hundreds or thousands of ideas. In short, the best ideas come from the employees on the front lines. And it takes humble leaders to accept this premise and act on ideas that don't originate from the executive leadership team.

Fast-forward to 2020, when I was searching for another interesting guest for my podcast (*Looking for AND*). *Corporate Creativity* was right at eye level on my bookshelf, so I reached out to Alan Robinson, who promptly agreed to chat about how innovation works. Robinson reiterated that it was frontline employees who were the source of lots of great ideas, and he also informed me that we were talking about a book that was over 20 years old …

So, I picked up a copy of *The Idea-Driven Organization— Unlocking the Power in Bottom-Up Ideas* by Robinson and Dean Schroeder. It became evident while reading case study after case study about the nuts and bolts of setting up an idea system that this was hard work. In addition, developing and maintaining a frontline idea system requires placing enormous amounts of trust in employees, something humble leaders are more likely to do.

Robinson's step-by-step process and his case studies come from decades of experience consulting with leaders on innovation. He can usually tell how successful a project is going to be by paying attention to some seemingly small details when he visits an organization for the first time and begins to unpack the culture. He asks: Do the executives have much nicer chairs and extremely larger offices? Is there an executive dining area? Do the executives get to park closer to the building in covered lots while everyone else has to walk further and park in uncovered spaces? Perks like these send signals to the employee base that the executives are primary, that "those at the top know best," and you should "do what you're told." It's a recipe for creating a culture where ideas are only really shared in a top-down fashion.

"I am the greatest."—Muhammad Ali

OK, Ali was right and, of course, it was part show. He was both a boxer and an entertainer. Some say he wasn't just the best boxer of all time—he may have been the best athlete of the 20th century, period. So, it would be disingenuous for him to say, "Yeah, I'm an okay boxer." And I would be negligent if we didn't also talk about the downsides of humility.

I do believe that one of the "laws" of the universe is that too much of anything is almost always a bad thing. Not speaking up, in some studies, has led people to believe we are not confident enough to lead. Quite often, the managers of executives I coach share this feedback. There is something inherent in American culture about speaking up. Spending too much time "backstage" can create a perception that a leader has lost his confidence.

In *Give and Take—A Revolutionary Approach to Success,* author and researcher Adam Grant's research shows that many of the people at the lower levels of an organizational hierarchy are "givers." That is, they spend much of their energy and time serving the needs of others. Consequently, they become "doormats" and do not advance too far in their careers. (Grant's research also shows that many "givers" make great executives when they figure out how to balance their need to help others with making sure they meet their own personal goals.)

As for the third element of our definition of humility (being accurate in our assessment of our abilities), the research shows that setting higher goals often leads to higher levels of achievement. Sometimes, we might need to think more of ourselves. Being accurate about our abilities may cause us to pass up challenging opportunities. The trick (again) is context, knowing when to take on more risk and tackle a stretch goal.

Lastly, "being open to influence" can make us susceptible to the desires, wants, and values of others. As leaders, we are often balancing the needs of many stakeholders, and some of these stakeholders may not have the wisdom, experience, and data to merit having influence over us.

"It is important that we learn humility,
which says there was someone else before me who
paid for me. My responsibility is to prepare myself so
that I can pay for someone else who is yet to come."
—Maya Angelou

So, what did all that humility get Jalen Hurts besides a chance to sit on the bench at Alabama? After his junior season with the Crimson Tide, Hurts opted to transfer to the University of Oklahoma, where all he did was shatter the Sooners' single game passing mark … in his first game! In 2019, he had his most productive season in college and finished second in the Heisman Trophy voting. More importantly, he led his team to the Big 12 Conference championship and a place in the College Football Playoff.

As of the writing of this book, Hurts is a starting quarterback in the National Football League for the Philadelphia Eagles. In his first season, Jalen did not shatter any records and he only started four games, where the team went 1–3. His statistics were hardly impressive. With that said, my money is on Hurts to bounce back, lead his team to the best of his abilities and, most importantly, be a positive role model for kids (and adults!) everywhere.

Re-Thinking Humility

Chapter 3
Why Now?

"If you ain't first, you're last."—Ricky Bobby

Any Will Ferrell fan will recognize this quote from one of his more successful movies, *Talladega Nights—The Ballad of Ricky Bobby*. In it, Ferrell plays the part of Ricky Bobby, who begins the movie as a member of the pit crew of a NASCAR team. In one of the first scenes, he is coaxed into driving when the actual driver decides to take a break during a race to get a burger. Ricky reluctantly gets in the car and shows a natural talent for racing. After a good showing in his first race, he fumbles the television interview badly and is unable to speak because of fright.

Ricky then begins to win races and the adoration of NASCAR fans. He quickly evolves from the dedicated, bumbling, team-first pit crew member to an egotistical jerk. We also get to see him dominate his own teammate, the unassuming, loyal Cal Naughton Jr. Cal continually sacrifices himself so that Ricky can command first place. At one point, Cal asks Ricky if he could win just one race. Ricky responds with, "Yeah, but if you won, how am I going to win?"

Eventually, Ricky loses his spot as the top driver, as well as his wife and his home. The only thing missing is a dog getting run over …

The story of Ricky Bobby is not just a comedy. Ricky is a caricature of what often happens when "success" (or the perception thereof) is thrust upon an individual and ego dominates. At the same time, there are some powerful lessons from the story (and more than a few laughs!). This movie was released in 2006, one year before the release of the iPhone and the onslaught of social media. Imagine Ricky Bobby on Twitter—it's not a pretty picture.

Now, imagine your life without a smartphone and/or social media. Remember what it was like when you walked into a conference room with your colleagues or when your instructor sent the group on a break during corporate training. Remember what it was like to walk down the hall in your office and greet people without their heads buried in a device.

Prior to smartphones, we had no choice but to look within ourselves and consider our options when we were bored. Today, we often reach for our phones the second we get a free moment. Boredom (and the chance to actually address it) has vanished with these mesmerizing devices. As Sherry Turkle writes in *Reclaiming Conversation—The Power of Talk in a Digital Age*, human beings have virtually lost the ability to be bored. Remember when your parents took you on vacation as a kid and you just stared out the window for hours? Remember when your mom forced you outside to play with your friends instead of watching TV all day? What did we do? We engaged in conversation. We asked each other questions. We connected. We got creative. Now, people bury their heads in their phones so as not to miss an important email or text. Today, we disconnect and drift off into our own self-curated worlds.

Unfortunately, these absolutely amazing devices that fit in our pockets are harming us in at least two ways. First, they are addictive. Second, they inhibit conversation. According to Turkle's research, anticipating a message releases the same chemicals into our bloodstream as that of a gambling addict when he is about to receive an additional card from the dealer. If you're interested in conducting a little experiment on yourself, try this: Leave your phone home for a day. Leave it when you go to the grocery store. Or, just leave it at home when you take a walk after dinner with your family. Count how many times you reach for your device or even think about all the messages you might be missing.

Did this experiment bring on a small dose of anxiety? Did you feel like you were missing out? If you answered yes to either of these questions, remember that there is an addictive element that powers almost all of the apps on your device. The algorithms powering these apps are gunning for your attention.

The second way that our mobile devices get us in trouble is by inhibition. As Turkle's research points out, when there is a smartphone within eyesight of two people having a conversation, they share less information. That is, "we" share less information. No one is immune to the distraction of a mobile device, and now that almost every human on the planet in the industrialized world above the age of six has one, we just don't speak to each other as much as we used to.

One of the scarier elements of Turkle's research shows that all of this heads-down tapping and swiping is having a negative effect on our ability to read other people. In some younger populations, empathy has dropped by roughly 40 percent. This means that the woman you just hired out of college may not understand or recognize it when you or your customers are angry, embarrassed, or sad. It means that we are losing our ability to care for one another and demonstrate compassion.

These sleek, powerful little devices are making us more selfish. It's just easier to send a text to someone on their birthday than make a phone call that could last five minutes. It's easier to "flame" someone on Twitter than to have a conversation where we ask questions, listen, empathize, and genuinely try to understand someone with a different point of view.

It's also incredibly easy to "humble brag" online. Several years ago, I had just finished a fun day of hiking with my two sons. My phone, of course, was out multiple times taking photos of the boys next to a big fallen tree they had pretended to knock over or just catching them doing something cute. I probably had two dozen pictures from our time together. Sitting down later that night after dinner, I reached for my phone and opened Facebook. Remembering all the great pictures on my phone, I rushed to post my favorites, then I waited. I waited for the Likes and the comments about what a great dad I was for spending time with my kids. Facebook on. Humility off.

**"It is well to remember that the entire universe,
with one trifling exception, is composed of others."
—John Holmes**

On March 11, 2020, the World Health Organization declared COVID-19, the disease caused by SARS-CoV-2, a pandemic. The announcement came after several months of reports about strict lockdowns in Wuhan, China, and medical professionals learning more about a new, potentially lethal virus that was rapidly spreading around the world. We all know how this is turning out.

As far back as 2009, researchers Jean Twenge and Keith Campbell were ringing the alarm bells about another epidemic. This one was different, though. You couldn't catch it from a sneeze or a cough. You couldn't get a vaccine for it, either. And, the test for it is a 40-question psychological assessment. Narcissism, the researchers argued, was on the rise to the point of it being an epidemic.

The American Psychological Association defines narcissism as a personality disorder with the following characteristics: (a) a long-standing pattern of grandiose self-importance and an exaggerated sense of talent and achievements; (b) fantasies of unlimited sex, power, brilliance, or beauty; (c) an exhibitionistic need for attention and admiration; (d) either cool indifference or feelings of rage, humiliation, or emptiness as a response to criticism, indifference, or defeat; and (e) various interpersonal disturbances, such as feeling entitled to special favors, taking advantage of others, and inability to empathize with the feelings of others.

While this epidemic is not taking lives and stressing our healthcare system, it is harming our ability to collaborate, innovate, and develop trusting relationships.

In *The Narcissism Epidemic—Living in the Age of Entitlement,* Twenge and Campbell share a number of data points that have convinced me that we do, in fact, have a problem. Some of the most compelling evidence, however, comes from a made-up scenario from the authors. Consider a situation that many of us over the age of 40 can probably relate to in some way or another. When we were kids and we did something wrong, our mothers might say something like, "Who the heck do you think you are?" The message was obvious: *You are not so special that you get to break the rules.* On top of that, our parents were not afraid to show their anger toward us for our transgressions. It didn't feel very good to have Mom or Dad raising their voices a bit, and it was how we learned what not to do. In fact, the research is pretty clear on this. If you want to stop a behavior, consider an appropriate punishment. If you want to encourage a specific behavior, consider an appropriate reward.

In contrast, many parents today might say as evening rolls around, "What do you want for dinner?" The difference is stark. So much of today's "helicopter" parenting is focused on making sure our kids don't feel bad or left out. They feel so good, in fact, that we're breeding a nation of narcissists who look out for themselves and break down in tears when their managers give them negative feedback. One human resources manager told me that helicopter parenting has moved from the soccer field to the office. It is not uncommon for the parents of recent college graduates to show up at first interviews, attempt to negotiate salaries, and even confront managers who hand out lower-than-expected performance ratings!

This "me-first" culture isn't just about kids and recent college grads. In 1980, the average CEO earned forty times that of the lowest-paid employee. Today, that ratio is 325:1. This is simply unfair. Yes, a great CEO can turn a company around. The CEOs I know work incredibly long hours and make incredible sacrifices. And, an economist may argue, we live in a capitalistic society where the market dictates these terms. All true. Except, it's still not fair and it really does not represent the fact that CEOs don't make decisions in a vacuum. They rely on others for information, guidance, and follow-through. No wonder a recent Gallup poll on trust found business executives close to the bottom.

"Yup, flying through the air. This is not good."
—Ricky Bobby

Talladega Nights (spoiler alert!) finishes with Ricky and his best friend reuniting. Ricky gets the geeky, educated girlfriend and his family gets back together. His best friend even gets to experience the winner's circle. A very happy ending. And, while Ricky Bobby is a fictional character, his story still resonates. He got a dose of humble pie when he lost his status as the number-one driver. It changed the way he treated other people, and he even apologized to his teammate for treating him poorly.

Power need not corrupt. Fame, accomplishment, and recognition do not have to end in arrogance, inflated ego, and narcissism. The flip side of all this arrogance and narcissism can be too much humility. We'll tackle this delicate balance in the next chapter.

Re-Thinking Humility

Chapter 4
What About Too Much Humility?

**"You're never as good as everyone tells you when you win,
and you're never as bad as they say when you lose."
– Lou Holtz**

"Jen is just too humble," her manager told me. She then continued with, "This young woman has been a fantastic employee since day one. She just came in, put her head down, and went to work. She accepted everything we threw at her and she consistently overdelivered for our clients. But she refuses to take credit for her great work. She tells the partners that her team should get all the credit. I want the partners to know that team wouldn't be performing if they didn't have Jen leading it."

Jen's manager shared more thoughts for another couple of minutes. She gave me examples of how organized Jen can be, how detail-oriented she is and how much she cares about her team. All of these were strengths Jen was leveraging to get the most out of her team and win over clients. Jen's manager finished with, "But, gosh darn it ... I just want to see her be a little less humble." When I asked her why Jen needed to be *less* humble, the manager said it was so she could get promoted to partner. She felt that the firm was more likely to reward her with a partnership if she "acted more like a leader."

In another client coaching conversation, a different manager at a top biotech company said something similar to me about someone on his team. "I'd like to see Sunil speak up more in our staff meetings. He keeps using 'we' when he explains his decisions—I want him to take credit for his decisiveness and the quality of his decisions. He is way too modest."

I asked Sunil's manager to explain his rationale. He had a similar opinion to Jen's manager—*if you want to get promoted, you've got to be seen and heard by more people.* In addition, Sunil's manager felt that being "center stage" was a characteristic of great leaders. He thought that Sunil was too quiet to be an effective leader.

Jen and Sunil represent two misconceptions about humility. Let's talk about Jen first. She was a bright, affable, competent consultant who was promoted quickly. In my first conversation with her, I could tell she was uncomfortable about something. She was clearly holding something back and seemed hesitant to talk about moving to the next level. The more we spoke, the more it became evident to both of us. Jen wasn't too humble. She was just lacking confidence.

At first blush, someone might not readily see the difference between humility and confidence or why it's even worth pointing out. It's definitely worth discussing, because telling someone who is lacking in confidence to "toot their own horn," "speak up more," or "make sure other people know what you've accomplished" is the wrong way to help. Confidence and humility are two different concepts and are not mutually exclusive.

"You are what your record says you are."
—Bill Parcells, retired National Football League head coach
and member of the Pro Football Hall of Fame

A look at Figure 1 tells the story of confidence and humility. Low Confidence and Low Humility are a recipe for an unsatisfying life. Someone in Quadrant 1 obsesses with comparison. He is constantly evaluating himself against others and coming up short in his own mind. He does not believe he is competent, and he's also not willing to let anyone in on it. On the outside, this person is all bravado. He is quick to tell others about his accomplishments, ignore advice from colleagues, and focus on his own needs instead of what he could do to help the team. He expends a tremendous amount of time and energy in marketing himself as incredibly competent in all areas. Over time, his performance is seen for what it really is and his selfishness makes it difficult to form trusting, long-lasting relationships with others. If he is charming, he bounces from company to company until he wears out his welcome.

Figure 1

	Low Humility	High Humility
Low Confidence	Quadrant 1 *Draining Uncertainty*	Quadrant 2 *Long-Suffering Acceptance*
High Confidence	Quadrant 3 *Shameless/Blatant Arrogance*	Quadrant 4 *Quiet Self- Assurance*

Jen was squarely in Quadrant 2. This was hard for others to understand because she did great work. Confident people sometimes have trouble understanding this. When you're confident, it makes sense to you that everyone thinks this way. Yet it is possible to misinterpret the third element of humility (accurately assessing one's own abilities) and think less of yourself. It's also difficult to be confident if you were raised in a home where your parents were really good at pointing out your mistakes. Many people low in confidence also live in fear. They feel that overestimating their abilities is a recipe for disappointment. Therefore, they aim low and are never disappointed.

Psychologists like to refer to confidence as self-efficacy: "an individual's belief in his or her capacity to execute behaviors necessary to produce *specific* performance attainments" (italics mine). The standard dictionary definition of confidence looks something like this: "belief in oneself and one's powers or abilities." The difference between the two is subtle. When we put time and energy into increasing our competence in a specific task or skill (e.g.: public speaking, giving feedback, asking questions, listening), growth in this area will naturally lead to higher levels of self-efficacy. On the other hand, self-confidence is a less specific, more general way of thinking about ourselves and others. If I observe Jen in a meeting where she doesn't speak up as often as I'd like, I may think it is her lack of confidence (or too much humility) when, in fact, it quite possibly could be that she never learned how to speak in public. And, giving someone constant feedback in the form of "You need to be more confident" or "less humble" leaves this person wondering what they're doing wrong with no clear strategies to address it. (Chapter 6 is all about strategies and tools to address this challenge/dynamic.)

It's no fun to have a Quadrant 3 person on your team. Arrogance (high confidence and low humility) lays the foundation for a competitive team culture, and not the good kind. People who demonstrate arrogance tend to seek attention, focus solely on their own needs, overestimate their abilities, and disregard the input of others. They may not be all of these things at once, and it is possible that only two or three of these dominate. In either case, arrogance chips away at the connection between human beings and fosters behaviors that are detrimental to collaboration and creativity.

Quadrant 4 is where we find the servant leader. This is Sunil. He had steadily climbed up the corporate ranks over the last thirty years. He was competent, full of wisdom, generally likable, and incredibly hardworking. Sunil had so many frequent flyer miles that his family rarely paid for flights. He was taught humility as a virtue early in his life. His parents often brought big decisions to the rest of the family for consultation, and he was taught to avoid the spotlight and bragging. Sunil craved input when making decisions and did not hesitate to change his mind when presented with strong arguments and incontrovertible data that disproved his hypothesis. After three decades of work in his field, he knew his strengths and weaknesses. It was rather easy for him to ask for help in his areas of weakness and focus on his strengths. In short, he was comfortable in his position and confident overall.

Sunil's manager saw it a different way. He saw Sunil's humility as a weakness, not a virtue. This was a tricky situation because Sunil's manager (the CEO, by the way) had a very different set of values. His idea of a great leader looked a little like Russell Crowe in *Master and Commander,* where the leader has all the answers and barks them out loudly and confidently to save the day. In the end, Sunil decided to speak up a little more often. He had a number of heart-to-heart conversations with his manager and they were able to find a comfortable middle ground. Sunil was open to his manager's feedback and new ways of thinking and behaving. I'd like to think that both men grew from the experience.

"To go fast, go alone. To go far, go together."
—African proverb

Sometimes we need to go fast. Sometimes we need to put our interests first. Sometimes we need to believe our abilities are better than they actually are in reality. And sometimes we need to be stubborn and resist changing our minds.

This is the life of a leader. There are many gray areas to navigate. Humility is not a cure-all for every situation you face. The four components of humility represent guideposts that can help you craft a way of being that makes you more trustworthy, more likable, more highly respected, and more effective. It is a values-based philosophy for how you conduct yourself.

Chapter 5
Who Can Teach Us?

*"I now wish to make the personal acknowledgment
that you were right, and I was wrong."*
—Abraham Lincoln (in a letter to Gen. Ulysses S. Grant)

The short answer to "Who can teach us?" is "Anyone, every-one, and everything." We can learn how to be a little more humble when we don't get the promotion we expected. We can learn about humility from the little girl who is willing to give her last cookie to her friend just because she thinks it's the right thing to do. We can learn it on Saturdays, Sundays, and any other day of the week that we may worship. We can access our humility when the funeral procession makes us wait when we're in a hurry. The humility process is all around us. Life is humbling. Sometimes it's excruciatingly painful. Sometimes it's just a scrape on the knee or even a historic, transformational leader such Abraham Lincoln acknowledging to his commanding general that he was wrong.

Identifying paragons of humility is a tall task for several reasons. First, everyone has an ego and some level of desire to be recognized. The reality is that we all put our own needs first from time to time. In fact, if we didn't, we probably wouldn't see some of the inspirational achievements around us. Human beings are fantastic at overestimating their abilities, and we just don't like to be told we're wrong. No one is 100 percent humble 100 percent of the time, nor am I recommending that anyone strive for that.

The longer story is that each of us can be conceited, stubborn, self-centered, and boastful (hopefully, not all at once!). We all have the capacity to be humble and we all have the capacity to be arrogant. The people I will examine all have shortcomings, and some readers may completely disagree with the choices I have made. I respect that, and I only ask that you consider whether each person is a good example of one or more components of humility.

"When you are finished changing, you're finished."
—Benjamin Franklin

In 1963, Katharine Graham was 46 years old, the mother of four kids, and the wife of Philip Graham, the CEO of *The Washington Post*. For the previous twenty years, Katharine's focus had been raising the kids and maintaining the Graham home. One tragic day that year, her husband Philip—who suffered from deep depression—committed suicide. As any of us would be, Graham's world was shattered. Yet overnight amidst her horrific grief, Katharine Graham was made the President, and later CEO —the only female CEO in the *Fortune* 500 at the time. A naturally shy person, she was understandably intimidated and terrified by what lay before her.

What many don't realize is that during Katherine Graham's tenure, she led *The Washington Post* through a historic financial run. From the company's IPO in 1971 until her retirement twenty years later, the compound annual return for shareholders was a whopping 22.3 percent. She crushed the S&P index (7.4 percent) and outperformed the average CEO (12.4 percent) over the same period. In fact, a dollar invested in her company in 1971 was worth $89 upon her stepping down as the chairman of the board in 1993.

Graham helped guide *The Post* through a number of crises without begging to be in the spotlight. She made the final call to print the Pentagon Papers, an incredibly courageous decision. She guided editorial decisions regarding the Watergate scandal and numerous other choices that were victories for the First Amendment. Graham also made shrewd business decisions that ran counter to her peers at other major newspapers. For example, *The Washington Post* was late to the game with color printing. Graham held back until the equipment was more reasonably priced. Her decision did not adversely affect circulation. It did contribute to a healthier bottom line.

Graham also brought a little-known investor onto the board named Warren Buffett. He became a mentor of sorts and he undoubtedly influenced many of her decisions in a very positive way. She spent her last years as CEO grooming her successor and that of her trusted COO, Dick Simmons. Through it all, Graham did not seek the limelight. She didn't grab the microphone to share her opinion and show the world she was in charge. She focused on the health of the company, in the present and in the future. She avoided the distraction of the podium and made leading her number-one priority.

Another great example of the "quiet" CEO who led from behind is Pixar's Ed Catmull (he retired in 2019). Pixar's achievements are well documented. If you have a child, niece, nephew, grandson or granddaughter under the age of thirty, you know exactly what I'm talking about. Pixar's run of number-one movies is absolutely unprecedented. This streak will most likely never be equaled or beaten. Catmull was (and probably still is) one of the main reasons for Pixar's success.

Since founding the company, Catmull has focused much of his energy on getting the "right" people to come on board and driving a system and culture that makes continued success more likely. In the creative process of making a movie like *The Incredibles,* for instance, the story, dialogue, character design and animation go through continuous reviews. The employees responsible for making you laugh, cry, and sit in awe are putting their ideas out there for people to criticize. It's not easy to hear that the plot doesn't make sense or that Elastigirl's outfit is distracting. The feedback needs to be delivered in a way that it is motivating and ultimately improves the final product. Yet Catmull led the charge in making these sessions a safe place for the people that were most vulnerable. At one point, he removed the famous Steve Jobs from these meetings because of the negative effect he was having on the staff. It wasn't necessarily that Jobs' feedback was inappropriate or harsh. He was ... Steve Jobs. People were intimidated by his persona. Catmull knew the same could be said for himself. Over time, he put more emphasis on having his team work on the details while he focused on the culture and strategy. Nice work, Ed!

Edward Everett was a highly respected statesman who served the state of Massachusetts in the House of Representatives and the United States Senate in the mid-1800s. He also served as governor of Massachusetts and as secretary of state under President Millard Fillmore. Everett was considered a statesman and eventually became a sought-after orator. It was not uncommon for crowds that numbered in the thousands to listen to him speak for hours at a time.

In one particular case in 1863, he was summoned to a then little-known town in central Pennsylvania—Gettysburg. Just four months after the bloody Civil War battle took almost 8,000 lives, Everett was the featured speaker. He described the tragedy of the epically bloody battle with a mastery of the English language that was lauded as an appropriate honoring of all who fell during the three tragic days.

At the same time, another speech was widely panned at this same dedication ceremony. President Abraham Lincoln spoke for roughly three minutes and the now-famous *Gettysburg Address* came out to a whopping 271 words compared to Everett's speech, which was over thirteen thousand words in length. Shortly after the ceremony, Everett wrote to Lincoln and said, "I should be glad if I could flatter myself that I came as near to the central idea of the occasion, in two hours, as you did in two minutes." To which the humble Lincoln replied that he was glad his own speech was "not entirely a failure."

Lincoln could be known to go on for hours, as well. However, he knew when to be brief and resist the urge to make himself the focus. Seven hundred words and five minutes were all we got for his second inaugural address when the end of the Civil War was in sight and a deep fatigue had crept over the nation. Once again, at the critical moment, Lincoln chose brevity and modesty to convey the important messages of unity and forgiveness.

"The best way to find yourself is to lose yourself
in the service of others."
—Mahatma Gandhi

Nelson Mandela spent much of his life toiling away to bring equality to the people of South Africa. For decades, apartheid was the rule of law in his home country. Soon after Mandela earned his bachelor's degree, he began organizing protests to address the injustice of the horrific system of apartheid. Mandela's standing up resulted in his being jailed several times, and he eventually spent more than 27 years behind bars. On at least three separate occasions, Mandela rejected offers of a conditional release where he was asked to refrain from protests. He refused each time. He was tireless in the pursuit of ending white rule in South Africa.

When he was released from prison in 1990 by South African President F. W. de Klerk, Mandela immersed himself in talks with the government to end apartheid. Mandela did not fully trust de Klerk, yet he continued to work with him for the greater good. Eventually the two ended apartheid, and in 1994 Mandela was the first democratically elected president of South Africa. From very early on in his life and throughout his presidency, he dedicated himself to the principles of democracy—that all people have a right to vote and to a voice. Being true to his word, Mandela stepped down as president after just one term in office and put the country first.

Mandela exhibited other elements of humility. The following quotes are a lasting tribute to the man who endured so much for so many:

> *"I like friends who have independent minds because they tend to make you see problems from all angles."*

> *"A fundamental concern for others in our individual and community lives would go a long way in making the world the better place we so passionately dreamt of."*

> *"For to be free is not merely to cast off one's chains, but to live in a way that respects and enhances the freedom of others."*

> *"Resentment is like drinking poison and then hoping it will kill your enemies."*

> *"Lead from the back—and let others believe they are in front."*

While Mandela certainly put the needs of others before himself, he was not without personal drive and motivation. He did not shy away from the spotlight when necessary and, at times, he may have overestimated his abilities. This is why he is such a great example. He was human. He made mistakes. Yet he transformed a country and inspired the world.

Mandela is a great example of *Empathize & Focus on Others*. He is also well-known. The following example is a little less well-known and just as powerful.

Roberto Clemente was a Puerto Rican professional baseball player with the Pittsburgh Pirates from 1955 through 1972. At times he was crabby with the sports reporters who covered him and often said that he was the best right fielder in the game (and he was). Many times, Clemente would not chase fly balls over to the stands like most out-fielders do. He had seen enough fly balls to know which ones would stay in play and which would land in the stands. Still, many unfairly questioned his commitment to the team and labeled him as lazy.

There is no question, however, that Clemente had a big heart. He often spent much of his off-season helping less fortunate people in the Caribbean. In 1972, a massive earthquake ravaged the capital of Nicaragua (Managua). Clemente had visited the city just three weeks prior and almost immediately began coordinating relief supplies for the affected Nicaraguans. Upon hearing that the first several flights had been diverted by corrupt politicians, he decided to fly down himself with the latest supplies, hoping that his presence would help ensure the survivors of the earthquake received what they needed. Tragically, Clemente's plane crashed shortly after takeoff. He was rightfully inducted into the Baseball Hall of Fame the next year and Major League Baseball renamed *The Commissioner's Award* in his honor. It is now called the *Roberto Clemente Award* and it is given annually to "a player who demonstrates the values Hall of Famer Roberto Clemente displayed in his commitment to community and understanding the value of helping others."

Doug Hensch

*"The first principle is that you must not fool yourself
—and you are the easiest person to fool."*
—Richard Feynman

There are thousands of humble leaders to show us the way and many more examples that we could analyze, including Mahatma Gandhi, Mother Teresa, George H. W. Bush, and Marcus Aurelius. We could look at the thousands of healthcare workers who came to work every day without adequate protection from COVID-19 for much of the pandemic. We could honor our teachers who did their best to serve our children under difficult circumstances and the cashiers who kept the grocery stores open while making minimum wage.

In addition, we can disregard the narrative that says leaders are only judged on results. The legacy of a leader is part of the mix. How a leader conducts herself is incredibly important to forming and maintaining a culture. In *First, Break All the Rules—What the World's Greatest Managers Do Differently*, Marcus Buckingham and Curt Coffman write that leaders are "on stage, every day." We remember if our manager said "Hi" to us yesterday morning, if he asked how our sick child was doing, and when he took credit for our idea.

Jim Collins, author of *Good To Great—Why Some Companies Make the Leap ... And Others Don't*, stumbled across an interesting point when looking at the different data points that helped companies improve their standing. He was surprised to find that humility seemed to be a core value of the best CEOs. He calls them

"Level 5" leaders. They exhibit modesty versus always looking to be in the spotlight. They focus on "getting the right people on the bus" (e.g., building strong teams) because they know they can't do it alone, and they open themselves to being influenced and to continuous learning and improvement. Possibly their most important contribution is setting their companies up for success when they are no longer running the show. Level 5 leaders put others first and are more likely to make decisions that benefit the long-term interests of their stakeholders. One Level 5 leader told Collins, "I want to look out from my porch at one of the great companies in the world someday and be able to say, 'I used to work there.'"

Becoming a Level 5 leader is not easy, and it doesn't happen overnight. It is, however, worth the effort. Next, we'll explore simple practices that can cultivate your humility and make you a more effective leader, parent, and team member.

Chapter 6
How Do We Get More Of It?

*"The single most valuable piece of advice coming
out of psychology is to consider the opposite.
Ask yourself why you might be wrong."*
—David Dunning

If you are still reading and still interested in applying just a little more humility to your life, you're in the right place! Before you read on, you may want to engage in a short self-awareness activity. We have developed a brief quiz to help you identify which area(s) of humility might be right for you to address. The quiz is made up of 16 statements. Your job is to determine how much each statement sounds like you, most of the time. Don't over-think this, and have a little fun with it. Whether your score is high, medium, or low is not important. What is important is cultivating the right amount of humility for the situation and circumstances in which you find yourself.

To complete the free quiz, just go to www.DRHleadership.com/humility

Once you complete the quiz, jot down your scores below for easy reference:

Heading backstage; desire/need to stay in background: _____

Empathize and focus on others: _____

List your abilities accurately: _____

Permit others to influence you: _____

If you want to take a strengths-based approach, dig into the areas where your scores are higher. If you believe the lack of humility is getting in your way, focus on the lower scores. It's up to you. All I ask is that you pick just one or two tips or tools to practice at first. Don't try to eat the whole elephant at once.

*Skill #1: **H**eading backstage; desire/need to stay in background*

1. What gets you out of bed in the morning? What motivates you? Explore your answers and whether you are trying to impress others. Look for deeper meaning in what you do and why you might be on this good earth. Think about a higher purpose where you serve something larger than yourself. Keep Steve Jobs' interview in mind where he talked about making your little "dent in the universe." Don't think you have to cure cancer or invent the next renewable energy source to save the planet (although that would be great!). Just find that one thing in which your unique combination of strengths, resources, and skills can make the world a better place.

2. Make it a habit to write down three questions before you attend a meeting at work. Get really curious about the topic

of the meeting. How might we solve this problem? Who can help us? What are we missing? What are we doing well? Being curious stymies our ego. It sends a message to others that we care about what they think, feel, and believe. It also puts the group in a position of dialogue and discussion. With regard to humility, it puts you in the background and gives someone else the chance to be the hero.

3. While we often feel that what we are posting on social media can be useful for others, many of our posts are self-serving. Run an experiment on yourself for one week. Don't post anything. Don't react or share anything either. Journal about this experience. How did it feel? What did you miss out on? How has your standing with peers, clients, and friends changed?

4. Take an improv class. Better yet, hire Bob Kulhan and his team at Business Improv (www.BusinessImprov.com). When executed with humility, improvisational comedy is fun, engaging and just plain amazing to watch. When watching it, I often ask, "How can they be this funny in the moment?" Well, one of the 'secrets' is to focus on others. The best improv comedians build on others' ideas and look for ways to make their teammates get the laughs. So, stop trying to be funny and stop focusing on what you need. Embrace a mindset of setting others up for success.

5. Consider those around you. Pay attention to their accomplishments. Praise them in a public way. Do not take any
   credit for what was done. BONUS: Do this for someone you
   don't like.

6. For just a moment or two, imagine if your sole purpose as a
   leader was to want the best for others. Think of this as your
   guiding purpose as you continue to manage, encourage,
   and help while staying in the background. Consider how
   you can do this on a daily or weekly basis.

7. Sometimes, we don't get the amount of credit we think we
   deserve. The next time this happens, don't say anything.
   Just allow someone else to get the credit. Sit with your feelings and be curious about the emotions you experience.
   Examine your expectations around what you believe will be
   the ramifications of leaving someone else with the credit.
   Reexamine this act and your expectations sometime in the
   future. How accurate was your prediction? What did you
   gain and/or lose by not speaking up?

8. Admiral John Richardson, Chief Naval Officer for the United
   States Navy from 2015 to 2019, served the United States
   with dignity, class, and modesty. When a mutual friend of
   ours recommended that I reach out to the admiral to discuss
   how humility impacts leadership, I jumped at the chance.
   In preparation for our discussion, I sent Admiral Richardson

the definition that I would be using as the backbone of the book. He quickly replied with "My working definition of humility is pretty basic, and comes from Carmelite spirituality: Humility is the recognition of the truth. It is being aware of, and accepting, the truth of who we are." Constantly try to seek "the truth" in your life, no matter how much it hurts.

9. During a discussion about humility, Admiral Richardson also offered this sage bit of wisdom, "Train yourself to be aware of your desire to be recognized, then suppress it." This is powerful advice for several reasons. First, it recognizes that we all have a need and a desire to be recognized. There is nothing wrong with this element of our humanity. Desires, wants, and needs, however, are not always what's best for us or the teams we lead. Don't beat yourself up for recognizing this in yourself. Second, the advice suggests how we may need to create a new habit. Most likely, you will notice the opportunity to "suppress it" more than once. Again, this is OK and a sign that we are all works in progress. Remember that when we become mindful of our thoughts and beliefs, they have less power over us.

10. Practice complimenting others. Continually look for opportunities to praise others for the work they have completed or the effort they are making. Be on the lookout for their accomplishments and be specific about what you admire in their efforts and accomplishments.

*Skill #2: **E**mpathize and focus on others*

"People don't care how much you know,
until they know how much you care."
—Attributed to Theodore Roosevelt

1. When we are over empathetic, we lose our sense of objectivity. This is *not* what we need from our leaders. Edward Hess and Katherine Ludwig, authors of *Humility Is the New Smart: Rethinking Human Excellence in the Smart Machine Age,* offer an interesting way to fight the urge to either not listen at all because we think the other person's point of view is ridiculous or because we are prone to being persuaded too easily. They write that we might want to consider "trying on" the other person's idea. This is analogous to trying on a piece of clothing to see how it looks on you and whether it fits. "Trying on" the other point of view allows you to "take it off" and still send a signal to the other person that you care enough to listen to them.

2. When we say that something is "awesome," we are telling the world that we think it is excellent, inspiring, and/or impressive. When we stand in awe of a sunset, an athletic performance, or our colleague's ability to stay calm in the face of conflict, we are opening ourselves to being modest. When we practice having a sense of wonder and beauty in the extraordinary (e.g., landing on the moon) or even that

which is commonplace (e.g., a sunset), it's pretty hard to feel self-important.

3. If you want to bore a research psychologist, start talking about gratitude. They may roll their eyes at you because it is one of the most studied emotions in recent years, so it's not very exciting. However, the benefits of practicing gratitude are noteworthy and too long to list here. In short, gratitude is (1) the *acknowledgment* of goodness in one's life and (2) the *recognition* that the source of this goodness is at least partially from outside of us. For the next seven days before you go to bed, write down three good things that happened to you during the day. Then, take several minutes (or as long as it takes!) to jot down some notes about what caused each of these good things to happen.

4. When an executive commissions a 360-degree report, she is asking a coach to gather anonymous feedback. This is one of the most useful tools out there for executive development, and inevitably there is some "bad" news in the form of a story about how an executive treated someone on their team poorly. In these cases, Marshall Goldsmith, author of numerous books on executive coaching, recommends the "apology tour." It's pretty simple. First, identify those you may have offended or treated poorly. Then, set up some time to meet with each person individually. Next, say, "I am sorry for (yelling, interrupting, insulting, with-

holding information, etc.)." Remember to be specific. Offer reparations that are commensurate with the offense. Then, shut up and let the other person have their say. It may be difficult to hear that they do not forgive you right away. This final step is critical if you really want to be a humble leader who demonstrates vulnerability and compassion. Finish by saying, "Thank you." If you are met with anger, insults, or a rehash of the entire incident, don't fight back or defend yourself. Just say, "Thank you."

5. One of the most effective ways to make a true connection with another person is by helping them feel heard and understood. Consider changing your mindset to be curious. Pay attention to your own behavior in conversations. How much do you talk versus how much the other person talks? Try counting to five or ten before responding to anything the other person says to give them room to continue. Think about coming up with some go-to questions for different scenarios, such as "Where did you grow up?" or "What do you do for fun?"

6. The bumper sticker "Commit random acts of kindness" got it partially right. Research shows that doing something kind for other people not only enhances our well-being by generating comfortable emotions, it may also improve our empathy. Dr. Barbara Fredrickson, an expert in the study of emotions, suggests that we do nice things for others AND

that we make it inconvenient for ourselves by making a whole day out of it, traveling some distance to serve others, or doing something that takes us away from our normal routine. When we let the older couple go in front of us at Starbucks, we feel good for a couple of minutes. When we use a cherished day off from work and drive several hours to a remote community to help rebuild a house or serve food, the positivity can last for days.

7. *Ted Lasso* on Apple TV+ is one of my favorite shows. He is the eternal optimist and someone with great instincts for servant leadership. Early in season one, Ted meets the team's equipment manager. Ted introduces himself and waits for the equipment manager (Nate) to share his name. After a couple of awkward seconds, Nate shares his name and says, "No one has ever asked me that before ..." Later Ted remembers his name by calling out "Nate the Great!" Nate is obviously touched by this and several other gestures by Ted. The point is that Ted treats just about everyone the same—like royalty. For one month, avoid looking at people's titles and positions. Treat everyone like royalty. Journal about your experience.

8. Great leaders are not a dime a dozen. And great leadership can be rare in some organizations. The effective humble leader deflects praise and offers up his team as the source of positive results. It's tempting to take credit for the accom-

plishments you drove to fruition. Consider replacing "I" with "we" the next time you talk about your successes. It's a simple shift in attitude and mindset that your team will notice. And, it's probably more accurate!

9. Management guru Peter Drucker was a prolific writer who helped convince leaders around the world that management was a distinct profession. It was not something that people could automatically master with no training or education. In one of his more famous quotes, he said, "Treat your employees like volunteers." It's an incredibly simple statement that when understood can make any manager pause and consider the ramifications. Volunteers show up and exert effort because they want to do so. Often, by paying someone a salary, we believe that their hearts and minds are in their work *because* of the paycheck. Drucker knew better. He knew that employees were people and needed to be treated as thinking, feeling human beings who want to be heard, understood, and appreciated. Consider adopting this frame of mind as part of your leadership approach and see what happens.

10. Conflict is a way of life. Disagreements happen within the best teams, the best marriages, and the best friendships. In all of these cases, "the best" do all they can to empathize, to consider how the other person is seeing the situation. And, we all have our moments when those uncomfortable feel-

ings move us to say or do something that is unproductive, mean, or hurtful. Humble leaders pause when confronted with less-than-productive behavior by asking, "What burden is this person carrying?" The humble leader shifts her attention from being offended to caring and showing compassion. While we may feel the impact of someone's anger or disrespect, our own humility can help us understand it may not be about us. We only see snapshots of most people, so getting curious about their world helps us manage through difficulties and bring the conflict back to respectful interactions.

*Skill #3: **L**ist your abilities accurately*

1. As a teenager, I remember being frustrated with high school one day and complaining to my parents. I said something to the effect of, "What's the point of school? I just want to get a job so I can make some money and get on with my life." My dad's response is as clear today as it was over thirty years ago, "The day I stop learning is the day I die." To this day, it's hard to find a day where my dad is not reading a book and sharing some tidbit of what he has learned. Self-improvement guru Stephen Covey calls this "sharpening the saw." Committing to lifelong learning is a great way of being modest by recognizing you don't know it all. It builds self-awareness and curiosity, which leads to more learning. The more we end up discovering through educating our-

selves, the more we want to learn—a virtuous cycle that leads to more and more knowledge!

2. One of the more humbling experiences for many executives is the moment they read their 360 report. A 360 evaluation is often conducted by a certified coach, who interviews a leader's manager, direct reports, peers, and internal customers to determine the leader's strengths and areas for development. It is one of the most effective ways to begin the process of improving one's leadership effectiveness. It takes a certain degree of humility to process and accept what others think of you. It's also one of the most effective ways to gauge the skill level of a leader. If you haven't had a 360, get one!

3. Are you suffering from a confidence deficit? Are you struggling to feel that you belong in a leadership role? That's OK, you're not alone. At one point or another, every leader suffers from a lack of confidence. One way to address this is the *Reflected Best Self* exercise developed by researchers at the University of Michigan's Ross School of Business. In short, identify 15–20 people who know you well. Ask them to tell you (an email will do) what they see as your top three strengths. Make sure they provide you with examples of each strength in action. Read through all the answers and acknowledge the fact that others see you as a valuable, productive person. Then, identify the themes (strengths)

in their writing. Craft a simple plan to incorporate these strengths into your daily routine.

4. Get a coach. OK, I'm biased about this, being a coach. With that said, a professionally certified coach acts as both an objective source of information and as a cheerleader who encourages clients to be comfortably uncomfortable. The best coaches start by being curious and helping clients come to their own realizations about how to approach the world. They also tell it like it is by "holding up the mirror" when clients are denying reality.

5. Get a mentor. While a good coach comes from a place of curiosity, a good mentor uses her experience to teach, motivate, and inspire. Mentors are great when you need advice. Infused in the relationship is humility and a willingness to learn from another person who has more experience than you. Select a mentor who will (like a good coach) tell it like it is and give you honest feedback. Go in with the following mantra: "Don't tell me what I want to hear. Tell me what I need to hear."

6. Goals are everywhere—in business, sports, politics, education, etc. Set a goal that is aligned with your values. Consider the age-old approach of describing the goal with the SMART acronym by making it Specific, Measurable, Attainable, Realistic, and Time-based. Make sure the goal is aligned

with your values. Identify which strengths you will apply to pursuing this goal. Consider the areas where you are not strong and who can help you. Build a "team" of people who can be resources for you in your quest. Finally, ask yourself, "What is it inside of me that might go wrong?" Then, create a plan for overcoming that obstacle.

7. Goals are great and necessary. They help point the way to where we want to go and can serve as motivation to get there. Habits are *how* we get there. There are a number of best sellers out there on the subject, and my favorite might be one of the lesser-known books on the subject, *Tiny Habits: The Small Changes That Change Everything* by B. J. Fogg, PhD. In short, Fogg's research shows that motivation drops over time and that making a habit easy is the best way to ensure that the activity becomes a habit. For instance, if you want to improve your empathy, consider asking yourself how someone else feels just once a day. As Fogg writes, make it "tiny." Over time, you will build your empathy. The other benefit is becoming more aware of what you can and cannot do. Remember, one of the goals for improving our humility is to know the truth about our abilities.

8. Self-awareness does not come easy to everyone. One way to begin examining your emotional and psychological capabilities is through emotionally expressive writing. James Pennebaker outlines this brilliantly in *Opening Up: The*

Healing Power of Expressing Emotions. Just write about your emotions and experiences for 15–20 minutes a day for three or four days. Don't hold anything back. He recommends doing this after facing some adversity, and the results are fantastic: less depression, more happiness, higher levels of resilience, and fewer doctor visits! You will gain insights into the patterns, triggers, and stories that help and hinder you when things don't go your way.

9. If your confidence is low, practice some self-compassion. So many of the leaders I work with are compassionate, caring, and empathic toward other people. They put their teams ahead of themselves. Their teams love them and they put in exceptional levels of effort as a result. These leaders can also be pretty tough on themselves. My advice: think about how the most caring adult in your life treated you with compassion as a child. Be like that adult with yourself and recognize it's OK to be imperfect, just like every other person that has ever lived, is living, or will live someday.

10. Take a strengths assessment. My favorite is free, and it's available at www.VIAcharacter.org. The assessment is based on rigorous research, and the site offers dozens of tips, tools, and insights to help you use your strengths effectively. The evidence is clear that people who embrace their strengths and find new ways to use them on a regular basis experience higher levels of achievement and well-being. As

it relates to humility, knowing your strengths is 25 percent of the battle! And humility is one of the 24 strengths identified by the VIA researchers. Don't be alarmed if it's not one of your top strengths. Just be more mindful and intentional about your humility, and this strength will get stronger!

*Skill #4: **P**ermit others to influence you*

1. Asking for advice can feel like we are telling the world that we are weak or incompetent. You have probably heard this before: *No one is perfect.* That includes you! Asking for advice has several benefits. First, it is an act of vulnerability which invites higher levels of trust. Others see you as human and are usually eager to reciprocate with some vulnerability of their own, which drives trust higher. Second, asking someone for advice elevates the other person's status. You are empowering them to be able to offer new options. Next, advice from others broadens your perspectives. More ideas mean more ways to solve a problem, which leads to higher creativity and innovation. Lastly, asking for "advice" in place of "feedback" has been shown to be more effective. By simply changing this one word in our vocabulary, we increase the amount of useful information that we receive from others.

2. The role of bias in our lives has become relatively mainstream in the last several years with our political polarization, news networks with agendas, anti-vaxxers, and anti-maskers.

Researchers have identified several powerful biases that have been proven to drive us away from making good decisions and inhibit our ability to solve complex problems. One way to combat these biases and increase our humility is through the simple practice of listing five reasons why something may have happened. Human beings are good at jumping to conclusions because of our biases, so the next time something goes wrong, pause and write down five (or more) reasons why this may have occurred. It's a quick exercise that increases your psychological flexibility in the face of missed expectations and activates the humility you may need to address the situation.

3. Another way to show your openness to suggestions is to run after-action reviews (AAR). Originally designed by the United States Army, they are just as useful for leaders in nonmilitary organizations. They can be highly structured or a quick conversation with members of your team to get curious about how a project or task was executed. One of my favorite ways to facilitate an AAR is to ask two simple questions. First, "What went well?" This is a good priming exercise (especially after the outcome was less than perfect). The team is challenged to look for positive aspects of the team's efforts, planning, and execution. It also builds positive momentum that can create a safe place for team members to share their thoughts on the next step. Second, ask them to complete this sentence, "It would have been even better if ..." Again, we're not hiding from the fact that some elements of this

went poorly; we're just framing it in a way that encourages people to speak up. The goal is to learn from what you did well and what went wrong. BONUS: Be the first to answer the second statement with where you messed up!

4. Speaking of messing up, listen to Dave Cooper, the retired Navy SEAL who was ultimately responsible for training the team that killed Osama Bin Laden in 2011. Cooper spent 25 years with the SEALs and gained a reputation for creating great teams. I had the great good fortune of meeting Dave to talk about humility. He argues that leading with humility is an essential element in building the relationships necessary for great teams because humility enables curiosity. Consider these tips and quotes as you practice opening yourself to the influence of others:

   - "Having one person tell another person what to do is not a reliable way to make good decisions."
   - Remember that you are in the business of creating leaders, so you can't just tell people what to do. Let them have influence over the decisions and problem-solving. Let them "practice" being leaders whenever they have the chance.
   - Try to replace orders with questions. Get your team thinking instead of just following commands.
   - Consider saying something like "Tell me what's wrong with this idea" or, "Now, let's see if someone can poke holes in this."

- Coop also recommends running your AARs immediately. Go in with the mantra of "rank switched off, humility switched on."

5. AARs, questions, and asking for advice are very direct ways of inviting others to influence you. Using tentative language is a more subtle and possibly more powerful way to accomplish this. When leaders use phrases like "My theory about this is ..." or "It might be interesting to try ..." or "I wonder if a possible solution could include ...," they are sending an indirect signal that they want the other person to contribute to the discussion. Tentative language opens the door for others to build on ideas and feel safe doing so.

6. The first time someone called me a "know-it-all," I cringed. (And, yes, there was a second and third time, unfortunately!) It's an insult and, in my case, it landed in a way that opened my eyes. We look at "know-it-alls" as arrogant people who can be disrespectful to teammates. One way to remind yourself of this is to make a list of all the things of which you are ignorant. Don't be shy; use as much paper or whiteboard as you need. Make the list long. Take a picture of it and maybe even send it to some trusted friends. Be sure to remember this list the next time you are "certain" that you have the right answer.

7. Have you ever said something like, "That guy makes me so angry" or "She just gets under my skin"? I'm pretty sure that

we have all uttered these words at one time or another. It's not helpful for a couple of reasons. First, you are implying that this person has power over you. Whether you are conscious of this or not, it probably just makes you feel angrier, sadder, or more powerless. Second, it's not accurate. Yes, there are some truly bad people out there who can be so mean that they do make people angry, sad, embarrassed, etc. However, the great majority of people we come in conflict with are just off their game, have a different point of view, or even have a different set of values. That doesn't make them bad people. Third, putting all the blame on someone else for our situation and/or our feelings positions you as the victim. Playing the role of a victim can become a bad habit that also reduces your ability to master your environment. So, instead of blaming, try asking, "What role did my actions or beliefs play in creating this situation?" This little dose of humility can help you get out of the downward spiral and start thinking about what you can *do* to improve the situation.

8. I'm convinced that humility, curiosity, and empathy are absolutely essential for great leadership. A fourth competency just may be creativity. Innovative solutions to today's problems might be the only way for us to attack some of the world's most difficult problems. And, while you may not personally be on the hook for figuring out how to end the political polarization in our society or solving the climate crisis, you will need to do

more with less, know how to create cohesive teamwork with employees who do not meet in person, and handle a myriad of other daily setbacks and challenges. The research is clear when it comes to creativity. When first setting out to find a creative solution, value quantity over quality. If you want to be a better problem solver and show others that you're open-minded, commit to generating a minimum of five explanations for every setback or problem. You will send a message to those around you that their ideas will be accepted and discussed, not rejected out of hand.

9. Generating lots of ideas is often referred to as "brainstorming." Hal Gregersen, PhD, saw that these brainstorm sessions often left a lot to be desired. (Check out www.LookingForAND.com for my conversations with Roger Firestien about *how* to run effective creative problem-solving workshops.) So, he came up with a new method for helping people get unstuck when confronting nasty problems. Gregersen calls it "question storming," and it goes like this. Get a small group of people to help you with your issue. Make sure that at least two or three of the participants are not members of your team and do not have much knowledge of your problem (their lack of knowledge helps them ask some of the basic questions you may be taking for granted, and they are much more likely to challenge your basic assumptions). When you have this group assembled, take no more than two minutes to share the outline of your issue. Then, have the group generate a minimum of 25 questions. There are

two rules: (1) No one can answer any of the questions. (2) No one needs to share *why* they are asking a particular question. The goal is to help you (the problem owner) think about the problem differently. Question storming doesn't usually lead to a new solution. It does, however, almost always generate new ways of seeing the problem and getting you unstuck.

Today's work environment is more inclusive than ever. In part, technology has made problem-solving more difficult and employees demand more of a say in how things get done. Add to that technologies like chat, shared drives, and smartphones, and it is easier than ever to collaborate. Like any good thing, it can feel like it's being overdone. Some of the more decisive leaders I work with can sometimes shy away from being more inclusive in their decision-making because it can be incredibly difficult to make everyone happy. The next time you have a big decision to make or you're leading an important project, take some extra time to think about the list of people, teams, and departments that may be affected by your actions. Reach out to them and let them know you would like to include them and that you value their input. PRO TIP: Include people who often disagree with you.

Epilogue
What Do We Do Now?

"Wisdom tells me I'm nothing. Love tells me I'm everything.
Between the two my life flows."
—Nisargadatta Maharaj

We live in dangerous, difficult, divisive times. We're facing raging wildfires, a pandemic that doesn't seem to want to go away, and political polarization that runs so deep that I'm pretty sure if you put a hard-core Democrat in the same room with a hard-core Republican, they would disagree on the color of the sky. And, before I go any further, I do not think that any one virtue, strength, or approach can solve complex problems such as these. With that said, we're doomed without a good dose of humility. It is the catalyst that we'll need from our leaders at every level and from citizens throughout the world.

So, imagine a future where we value humility more than we do today. Think of a time in the future when we have leaders who truly focus on others, maybe to the detriment of their own personal success. Consider a future where we have leaders who don't spend half of their day on Twitter or brag about their social media following. And, imagine a future with leaders who know themselves so well that they surround themselves with talent that fills in their weak spots and leaders who leave themselves open to being influenced so that we achieve greater success for greater numbers of people.

I have shared many of these ideas with friends, family members, colleagues, and clients. So far, no one is really pushing back. There is some skepticism, however, about turning this ship around. Remember that power is not gained by individuals, it is given by the masses. We can start demanding more humility from our leaders. We can also demand it from our kids, our teams, and ourselves. The next time you see someone bragging, putting their needs ahead of the many or refusing to listen to differing opinions, get curious with those around you. How is this behavior good for us? What is it teaching our kids? What would the effect on us be if this person were exhibiting humility?

Humility isn't just a nice thing to have because it is a universal virtue. It is an essential element of good leadership. Let's start that conversation and see where it goes.

Acknowledgments

A slightly overdue thank you is owed to my one-of-a-kind nephew, Brad Szoka. Brad executed some great research for my first book and was not acknowledged. (I'm hoping he actually reads this book before jumping to the Acknowledgments this time—ha!)

My sisters, Kathlene Szoka and Susan Ludwig, put me in my place more than once when we were kids. I still hear their voices telling me to be a little more modest. Thank you. I needed to hear that.

Nicholas and Zachary Hensch have been a source of joy and happiness from day one. Just as importantly, they have had to listen to me rant and rave about the lack of humility in our society (particularly when we watched sports). Thank you for enduring my obsession with this topic.

Ryan Galloway, Reese Galloway, and Valor Brignoli welcomed me and my boys into their family without hesitation and with open arms—a great example of "team first" where the example was set by the love of my life, Tammy Hensch. Thank you for enduring the nights and weekends of reading, researching, writing, and editing to get this puppy done!

A huge Thank You to Joel Nylund, Dave Cooper, Bob Kulhan, Alan Robinson, Jamie Millar, Barry Coleman, Lori Zukin, Brad Sterl, Anne Loehr, and Tony Nader for sitting through my interviews. Not only did they thoughtfully answer my questions, they patiently listened to my pontificating on this topic.

I wish the world had more leaders like Admiral John Richardson. Thank you for your service to our country and to humanity. You are an example for all of us, and I will always be grateful for your time and feedback.

If you need a coach or someone to help your organization take a strengths-based approach to its culture, just hire Shannon Polly. Shannon knows this stuff inside out. She went above and beyond to help me define this ancient virtue and find some great examples.

Paul Haefner is my go-to person for advice and counsel. More than once, Paul has shown me the way to being a more mindful, curious human being. His wisdom may know no limits (and I'm guessing he's laughing at me with that one!).

If you're interested in writing a book, look no further than Bethany Kelly. Bethany is the epitome of "honesty AND kindness." Without her knowledge, experience, and attention to detail, this book would never have been completed.

Once the book is written and you want to make it shine, look no further than Frank Steele. His edits were...amazing. Thank you, Frank, for bringing your expertise, curiosity and detail orientation to the book.

Somehow, Sissy Estes made humility come to life. She tirelessly made edits to the book covers at my request. I love this book cover, and Sissy gets 100 percent of the credit!

Daniel Porter was featured in my first book because of his inspiring level of resilience. Well, Daniel inspired me again. He read every word of the manuscript and offered sound advice and encouragement. I couldn't wait to hear back from Daniel after I sent him a chapter. He kept me on track and believing that this was an important project.

Only one person in this world gets to claim they have the World's Best Best Friend—that's me. Jim Hock has held this title for 39 years. He was with me from the moment I decided to write this book, to the outline, to the decision to hire a coach, and through every word on these pages. Jim went above and beyond to bring his expertise, passion, and intellect to every chapter. I cannot thank him enough.

Re-Thinking Humility

Sources

Chapter 1—What is humility?

C. S. Lewis quote: Aaron Armstrong. "What CS Lewis wrote is more powerful than what he didn't." Blog. December 11, 2015. https://bloggingtheologically.com/2015/12/11/what-cs-lewis-wrote-is-better-than-what-he-didnt/

Coyle, Daniel. *The Culture Code: The Secrets of Highly Successful Groups.* Bantam, 2018.

Marquet, L. David. *Turn the Ship Around!: A True Story of Turning Followers into Leaders.* Penguin, 2012.

Chapter 2—So What?

Baldoni, John. *Grace: A Leader's Guide to a Better Us.* Indigo River Publishing, 2019.

Edmondson, Amy C. *The Fearless Organization: Creating Psychological Safety in the Workplace for Learning, Innovation, and Growth.* John Wiley & Sons, 2018.

Emmons, Robert A. *Thanks!: How the New Science of Gratitude Can Make You Happier.* Houghton Mifflin Harcourt, 2007.

Grant, Adam M. *Give and Take: A Revolutionary Approach to Success.* Penguin, 2013.

"Humility is a key to high performance and effective leadership." Research brief. Foster School of Business, University of Washington. September 19, 2012. https://foster.uw.edu/research-brief/humility-is-a-key-to-high-performance-and-effective-leadership/

"Nick Saban Gets Choked Up Talking About Jalen Hurts Winning SEC Championship." YouTube. December 1, 2018. https://www.youtube.com/watch?v=2aZHe6An7J8

"No one has a story like Jalen Hurts." YouTube. January 16, 2019. https://

www.youtube.com/watch?v=XndDmmZQjGE

Polly, Shannon, and Kathryn Britton, eds. *Character Strengths Matter: How to Live a Full Life.* Positive Psychology News, 2015.

Robinson, Alan, and Sam Stern. *Corporate Creativity: How Innovation and Improvement Actually Happen.* Berrett-Koehler Publishers, 1998.

Chapter 3—Why now?

APA Dictionary of Psychology, s.v. "narcissism." https://dictionary.apa.org/narcissism

Mackey, John, and Rajendra Sisodia. *Conscious Capitalism: Liberating the Heroic Spirit of Business*, with new preface. Harvard Business Review Press, 2014.

McKay, Adam, Alex Wurman, Hal Willner, and Erik L. T. Calderaro. *Talladega Nights: The Ballad of Ricky Bobby.* Columbia Pictures, 2006.

Peterson, Jordan B. *12 Rules for Life: An Antidote to Chaos.* Penguin UK, 2018.

Saad, Lydia. "U.S. Ethics Ratings Rise for Medical Workers and Teachers." Gallup. December 22, 2020. https://news.gallup.com/poll/328136/ethics-ratings-rise-medical-workers-teachers.aspx

Sacasas, L. M. "The Questions Concerning Technology." The Convivial Society: Vol. 2, No. 11. June 4, 2021. https://theconvivialsociety.substack.com/p/the-questions-concerning-technology

Turkle, Sherry. *Reclaiming Conversation: The Power of Talk in a Digital Age.* Penguin, 2016.

Twenge, Jean M., and W. Keith Campbell. *The Narcissism Epidemic: Living in the Age of Entitlement.* Simon and Schuster, 2009.

Chapter 4—What about too much humility?

American Psychological Association. "Teaching Tip Sheet: Self-Efficacy." 2009. https://www.apa.org/pi/aids/resources/education/self-efficacy#:~:text=Self%2Defficacy%20refers%20to%20an,%2C%20behavior%2C%20and%20social%20environment

Dictionary.com, s.v. "confidence." https://www.dictionary.com/browse/

confidence

Diener, Ed, and Robert Biswas-Diener. *Happiness: Unlocking the Mysteries of Psychological Wealth*. John Wiley & Sons, 2011.

Grant, Adam. *Think Again: The Power of Knowing What You Don't Know*. Viking, 2021.

Greenleaf, Robert K. *Servant Leadership: A Journey into the Nature of Legitimate Power and Greatness*. Paulist Press, 2002.

Headlee, Celeste. "10 Ways to Have a Better Conversation." Filmed May 2015 at TEDxCreativeCoast. Video, 11:21. https://www.ted.com/talks/celeste_headlee_10_ways_to_have_a_better_conversation

Sutton, Robert I. *The No Asshole Rule: Building a Civilized Workplace and Surviving One That Isn't*. Business Plus, 2007.

Chapter 5—Who can teach us?

Baseball Reference, s.v. "Roberto Clemente." https://www.baseball-reference.com/players/c/clemero01.shtml

Buckingham, Marcus, and Curt Coffman. *First, Break All the Rules: What the World's Greatest Managers Do Differently*. Simon and Schuster, 2014.

Catmull, Ed, and Amy Wallace. *Creativity, Inc: Overcoming the Unseen Forces That Stand in the Way of True Inspiration*. Random House, 2014.

Collins, Jim. *Good to Great: Why Some Companies Make the Leap … and Others Don't*. Harper Business, 2001.

Goodwin, Doris Kearns. *Team of Rivals: The Political Genius of Abraham Lincoln*. Penguin UK, 2009.

Grant, Adam. *Think Again: The Power of Knowing What You Don't Know*. Viking, 2021.

Heath, Chip, and Dan Heath. *Decisive: How to Make Better Choices in Life and Work*. Random House, 2013.

Hess, Edward D., and Katherine Ludwig. *Humility Is the New Smart: Rethinking Human Excellence in the Smart Machine Age*. Berrett-Koehler Publishers, 2020.

Holiday, Ryan. *Ego Is the Enemy*. Elex media komputindo, 2019.

MLB Awards, s.v. "Roberto Clemente Award." https://www.mlb.com/awards/roberto-clemente

Sachs, Jonah. *Unsafe Thinking: How to Be Creative and Bold When You Need It Most*. Random House, 2018.

Stoler, Mark A. *George C. Marshall: Soldier-Statesman of the American Century*. Plunkett Lake Press, 2021.

Thorndike, William N. *The Outsiders: Eight Unconventional CEOs and Their Radically Rational Blueprint for Success*. Harvard Business Press, 2012.

Chapter 6—How do we get more of it?

Covey, Stephen R. *The 7 Habits of Highly Effective People: Powerful Lessons in Personal Change*. Simon and Schuster, 2013.

Coyle, Daniel. *The Culture Code: The Secrets of Highly Successful Groups*. Bantam, 2018.

Emmons, Robert A. *Thanks!: How the New Science of Gratitude Can Make You Happier*. Houghton Mifflin Harcourt, 2007.

Fogg, Brian J. *Tiny Habits: The Small Changes That Change Everything*. Eamon Dolan Books, 2019.

Fredrickson, Barbara. *Positivity*. Harmony, 2009.

Goldsmith, Marshall. *What Got You Here Won't Get You There: How Successful People Become Even More Successful*. Profile Books, 2010.

Gregersen, Hal. *Questions Are the Answer. A Breakthrough Approach to Your Most Vexing Problems at Work and in Life*. Harper Business, 2018.

Hess, Edward D., and Katherine Ludwig. *Humility Is the New Smart: Rethinking Human Excellence in the Smart Machine Age*. Berrett-Koehler Publishers, 2020.

Oettingen, Gabriele. *Rethinking Positive Thinking: Inside the New Science of Motivation*. Current, 2015.

Patterson, Kerry, Joseph Grenny, Ron McMillan, and Al Switzler. *Crucial Conversations: Tools for Talking When Stakes Are High*. McGraw-Hill Education, 2012.

Pennebaker, James W. *Opening Up: The Healing Power of Expressing Emotions*.

Guilford Press, 1997.

Roberts, Laura Morgan, Jane E. Dutton, Gretchen M. Spreitzer, Emily D. Heaphy, and Robert E. Quinn. "Composing the Reflected Best-Self Portrait: Building Pathways for Becoming Extraordinary in Work Organizations." *Academy of Management Review* 30, no. 4 (2005): 712–736. https://doi.org/10.5465/amr.2005.18378874

Roberts, Laura Morgan, Gretchen Spreitzer, Jane Dutton, Robert Quinn, Emily Heaphy, and Brianna Barker. "How to Play to Your Strengths." *Harvard Business Review* 83, no. 1 (2005): 74–80.

Yoon, Jaewon, Hayley Blunden, Ariella Kristal, and Ashley Whillans. "Why Asking for Advice Is More Effective Than Asking for Feedback." *Harvard Business Review*, September 20, 2019. https://hbr.org/2019/09/why-asking-for-advice-is-more-effective-than-asking-for-feedback

Re-Thinking Humility

84

Made in the USA
Middletown, DE
07 October 2022